UPDATED GUIDE TO CREATING LOVABLE MARKETING CAMPAIGNS

Roman Bodnarchuk, N5R.com

Magdalena Georgieva, HubSpot

As a Toronto-based agency, N5R.com has over 14 years experience bringing exclusive digital marketing and lead generation management solutions to bear on sales campaigns for the world's largest brands, including **Apple, P&G, Johnson & Johnson, Hersheys, Nissan, Four Seasons, Ritz-Carlton, Hyatt, and Trump**.

With its global reputation for lead generation, N5R.com's momentum in inbound marketing has made it the #1 HubSpot partner in Canada.

When we saw HubSpot's recent launch of HubSpot 3, we couldn't help but put together this special edition of **Creating Lovable Marketing Campaigns**. The revolutionary software boasts a variety of tools – some new, some improved – to help you manage all your online leads in one place.

N5R.com will help transition your business to HubSpot 3 and manage your account so you can hit the ground running – before your competitors do.

Share This Ebook!

WWW.N5R.COM

HUBSPOT 3'S ALL-IN-ONE
MARKETING SOFTWARE

... brings your whole marketing world together in one, powerful, integrated system

- **GET FOUND: HELP PROSPECTS FIND YOU ONLINE**
- **CONVERT: NURTURE YOUR LEADS AND DRIVE CONVERSIONS**
- **ANALYZE: MEASURE AND IMPROVE YOUR MARKETING**
- **PLUS MORE APPS AND INTEGRATIONS**

Request A Demo   **Video Overview**

LEAD
GENERATION

BLOGGING &
SOCIAL MEDIA

EMAIL &
AUTOMATION

SEARCH
OPTIMIZATION

LEAD
MANAGEMENT

MARKETING
ANALYTICS

Share This Ebook!

N5R

WWW.N5R.COM

CONTENTS

••

Share This Ebook!

Why should you care about *Lovable* Marketing?

Simply put, because it works.

When people respond to your marketing time and time again, you know you've created something that they love. It means you've taken proper care to nurture your brand by providing content that is:

- **RELEVANT** – satisfies an information need

- **TIMELY** – engages audience when they are most responsive

- **FOCUSED** – engages the right audience

- **CONSISTENT** – maintains established level of user experience

Now take a moment.

Take stock of what works, because everything you know and love about noble marketing remains as relevant as they did five years ago.

What has changed is the complexity of marketing online.

The reality of social media has provided businesses more opportunities to interact with users. At the same time, the general user has become more tech savvy, more independent, and more selective in the types of communication they respond to.

The challenge is that the dynamic isn't going to end soon.

But with HubSpot 3, we're pleased to announce a much easier way for you to make to sense of what your leads are really telling you, so you can focus on what matters most: making Lovable Marketing.

Share This Ebook!

   ••••••••••••••••••••••••••••• N5R

HUBSPOT 3

The recent launch of HubSpot 3 is a centralized, synergistic approach to managing your customer relationships in a single database, called Contacts. Its most powerful application is in its ability to fully customize online user experience.

We aren't just talking about simple suggestion boxes here, folks.

With HubSpot 3, every time a new lead visits your website, Contacts tracks how that lead interacts with you, then begins building a dynamic profile that shapes all future communications with that lead specific to its stage in the decision-making process.

Much like the rest of HubSpot's built-in tools, this added functionality is engineered to keep your processes lean, powerful, and accessible.

N5R.COM: CANADA'S #1 HUBSPOT PARTNER

Lean, powerful, and accessible – few agencies in Canada understand that more than N5R.com, a small-sized firm based in Toronto, Ontario. As a leading social media marketing agency for more than 14 years, N5R.com has delivered successful marketing campaigns both on- and off-line for North America's biggest brands.

This updated step-by-step eBook on making lovable marketing is made possible by N5R.com in partnership with HubSpot. So put on your comfy shoes. We would love for you to join us on this journey.

Share This Ebook!

WWW.N5R.COM

HOW TO START MAKING LOVABLE MARKETING

In this ebook, N5R.com will show what you need to do in order to make a holistic marketing campaign, how HubSpot 3 tools can help you achieve it, and how N5R.com can make your life even easier by doing it for you.

From industry best practices and experience, here are some basic components of a successful marketing campaign:

- **PRODUCE A COMPELLING MARKETING OFFER**
- **PLACE THE OFFER ON YOUR WEBSITE**
- **ATTACH THE OFFER TO AUTOMATED WORKFLOWS**
- **PROMOTE IT VIA EMAIL, BLOG & SOCIAL MEDIA CHANNELS**
- **MEASURE RESULTS**

Each component of this campaign needs to carry the characteristics of marketing that people will love. Now let's start making successful and noble campaigns!

Share This Ebook!

1 DEVELOP A MARKETING OFFER

2 PLACE OFFER ON YOUR WEBSITE

3 BUILD AUTOMATED WORKFLOWS

4 MARKET TO YOUR EMAIL CONTACTS

5 PROMOTE THROUGH BLOG & SOCIAL

6 MEASURE THE IMPACT OF ALL ELEMENTS

CHAPTER 1

DEVELOP A STELLAR MARKETING OFFER

"*Think like a publisher.*"

Before you even think about all the confusing marketing tools out there – we know because we've used them to create lots of online campaigns for N5R.com clients – just pause and remember that all campaigns should be built on a solid marketing offer. Namely, it needs to satisfy the first characteristic of marketing that people love:

● EDUCATIONAL & HELPFUL

Constantly coming up with new content ideas, however, can be overwhelming. To handle the demands of content creation, marketers have been told again and again to "think like a publisher." It's great advice, but what exactly does that mean? Just how do you think like a publisher?

Like publishers, inbound marketers must have a detailed picture of their target audience in order to create optimal content for them.

Share This Ebook!

Focus on the Right Stage

Content plays a critical role in every stage of the inbound marketing process, from generating awareness about your company to helping convert leads into customers. But the types of content you should use to achieve each of these goals are often very different from each other.

AWARENESS

The prospect gets acquainted with your brand or realizes they have a need for your product/service.

RESEARCH/EDUCATION

The prospect identifies the problem and researches potential solutions, including your product/service.

COMPARISON/VALIDATION

The prospect examines the options and begins narrowing the list of vendors.

PURCHASE

The prospect decides from whom to buy.

Share This Ebook!

WWW.N5R.COM

N5R

N5R.com TRUMP CASE STUDY: Building Awareness

In 2012, N5R.com was tasked with a challenge: how to build awareness for a client who had no previously existing video showing their final product, which was already finished.

Client: Trump International Hotel & Tower® in Toronto.

Realizing we had to get the word out fast, N5R.com immediately went to work by creating a cross-media sales video that ran on the new sales show suite, on the website and online, and on the hotel channel for 24 hours a day, 7 days a week.

N5R.com also launched a website using the HubSpot platform. Here's some of what we delivered on:

•••••● **SEARCH ENGINE OPTIMIZATION:**

executed link-building and keyword targeting to improve SERP ranking of the Trump website

•••••● **WEBSITE ANALYTICS:**

identified which sources generated the most leads

•••••● **BLOGGING & SOCIAL MEDIA:**

created a blog to help transition leads all the way to the purchasing stage of the campaign.

Share This Ebook!

   ••

WWW.N5R.COM

What Content Attracts Traffic & Leads?

Content plays a critical role in every stage of the inbound marketing process, from generating awareness about your company to helping convert leads into customers.

But the types of content you should use to achieve each of these goals are often very different from each other.

••••••••• FINDING THE RIGHT TOPIC

In order to find what content topics capture the attention of your target audience, you should look at past data that you have access to. For instance, what are the most popular blog articles you have published?

What are some of the most viewed pages on your website?

Your historical performance should dictate your direction for new marketing content. If you don't have access to marketing analytics that give you this type of intelligence, look in the public domain (Google news, Google trends, Twitter trending topics) for popular and newsworthy industry stories. Piggyback on this information by adding a personal spin, your expertise and comments.

TIP: **N5R** **SEO - Content Marketing**

A study in 2011 by SEOmoz concluded that content marketing – a combination of inbound links, keyword usage, social media, and brand popularity – has an 82% impact on your SERP. Takeaway: content marketing is currently the best strategy for inbound marketing.

Share This Ebook!

● FINDING THE RIGHT FORMAT

You can create content in different formats, from text-based content like whitepapers, reports and ebooks to media content like webinars, videos and audio interviews. While you can host an internal brainstorm session and come up with creative ideas for different content formats that you can produce, it's important that this new content matches the needs and preferences of your target persona.

N5R.com recommends using HubSpot's Landing Page Analytics – it's a great tool to measure how all of your different types of content are contributing to your marketing campaign (i.e., what works when converting visitors to leads? What's the conversion rate?) It helps give your business an idea of which format to pursue – use it to build your marketing campaign around it.

Share This Ebook!

WWW.N5R.COM

CREATE VALUABLE CONTENT THAT YOUR PROSPECTS WILL LOVE

Will give you all the tools you'll need to create marketing that your prospects will love. Your content will be optimized for search engines, social media and ready to convert visitors into leads in minutes.

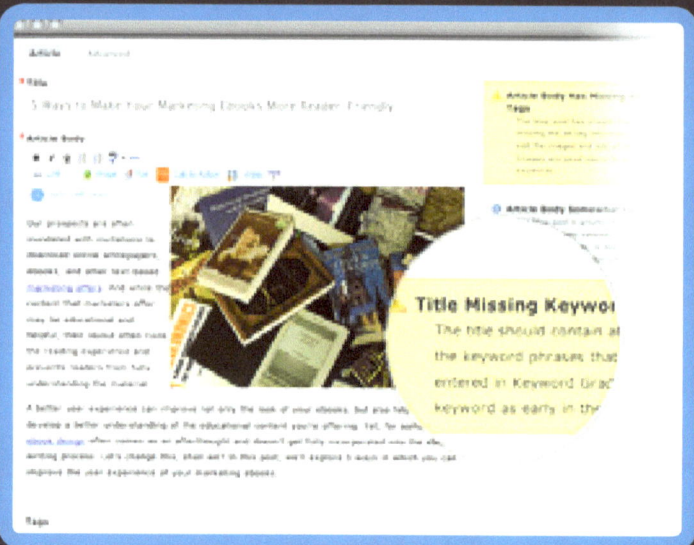

✔ Find out what keywords bring you the most traffic and have the least difficulty.

✔ Easily create optimized blog articles, website pages, and social media messages.

✔ Use one of Hubspot's content apps to get your blog posts delivered right inside your Hubspot account.

Request a Demo

Read More

Recruit a Team of Content Creators

When we're busy trying to engage our audience, we often have to remember to engage ourselves. Folks from all parts of your organization often have different perspectives on the same challenge: Technical folks, customer service people, C-level executives, product managers, and others can have opinions that improve your company's inbound marketing content. Engage your coworkers by:

• ● **Asking them to cowrite a whitepaper or an ebook.**

• ● **Interviewing them and posting short videos that share their expertise**

• ● **Inviting them to give presentations or answer questions in webinars**

HubSpot 3 makes it easier than ever before to write an ebook, but at N5R.com we understand the challenge that companies face when they make the move to migrate to a new technology. When it comes to transitioning to HubSpot 3, N5R.com can do for you what you need HubSpot 3 to do, without the learning curve – saving you time while propelling your marketing campaign in ways you've never experienced.

Share This Ebook!

If your organization doesn't want to go in-house for your content, you can try looking outside for help. Lots of new online content marketplaces are available for you to connect with freelance writers and editors who will take on your blog posts, ebooks, and other writing jobs – simply specify the topic, your desired style and tone, and your intended audience, and you typically don't have to pay unless you accept the finished article.

TIP: **N5R** **Crowdsourcing** Crowdsourcing can be efficient under the right circumstances, and with the right marketplaces, but beware if you're seeking quality copy for your important advertising needs. Make sure the content is relevant and unique from the other content out there, otherwise search engines could find and penalize your page ranks. If original sales copy is what your business needs, consider N5R.com – we've only been doing this for 14 years.

Share This Ebook!

   •   **N5R**

Repurpose Content

Here's a neat trick for bloggers: take key points from your existing material and use them to generate new blog posts.

Almost every piece of content you create can be updated, adapted, modified and republished in another format. Make a habit of finding multiple ways to package and distribute the same information in different formats – as long as remember to add value each time.

TIP: **N5R** **SEO – Repurpose, repurpose**

Repurposing content is a useful practice, but take care repurposing across different pages on the same domain: you may run the risk of "cannibalization" (i.e., own pages competing with each other for ranking) and risk being penalized by Google for duplicate content. Consider using the rel=canonical tag in your HTML to let Google know which page is your "official" page.

Here are a few ideas on how to repurpose your content:

- **Combine text from an old whitepaper** with new videos to create a multimedia ebook.

- **Turn videos or webinars into blog posts** and ebooks or vice versa.

- **Use commonly asked questions** and comments from webinars to create a new ebook. These topics will directly address your prospects' pain points.

- **Share all company presentations** in multiple formats. Post the slides on SlideShare, upload the video on YouTube, and create a series of blog posts that dive into specific points of the presentation.

At N5R.com, we've been doing this for years. For a look at slides of our presentations to Danier Leather, FORD Canada, and Proctor & Gamble visit our website at www.n5r.com. Pay close attention to how every presentation offers something different to each client, then imagine all the ways that repurposing content can help you drive traffic to your business.

Share This Ebook!

CHAPTER 2

PLACE OFFER ON YOUR WEBSITE

> **❝Your office is one part of an information exchange; the other part is the contract details of your visitors❞**

In order to start generating new leads from your offer, you need to place it on your website. You will do that by creating a landing page, a web page that features a description and an image of the offer and a form for visitors to fill out in order to receive the resource.

This transaction is type of an information exchange, in which the visitor gets the offer they are interested in and you receive the contact information of your visitors. They transition into their next lifecycle stage, that of leads.

This is the process of lead generation.

Share This Ebook!

WWW.N5R.COM

Lead Generation Visualized

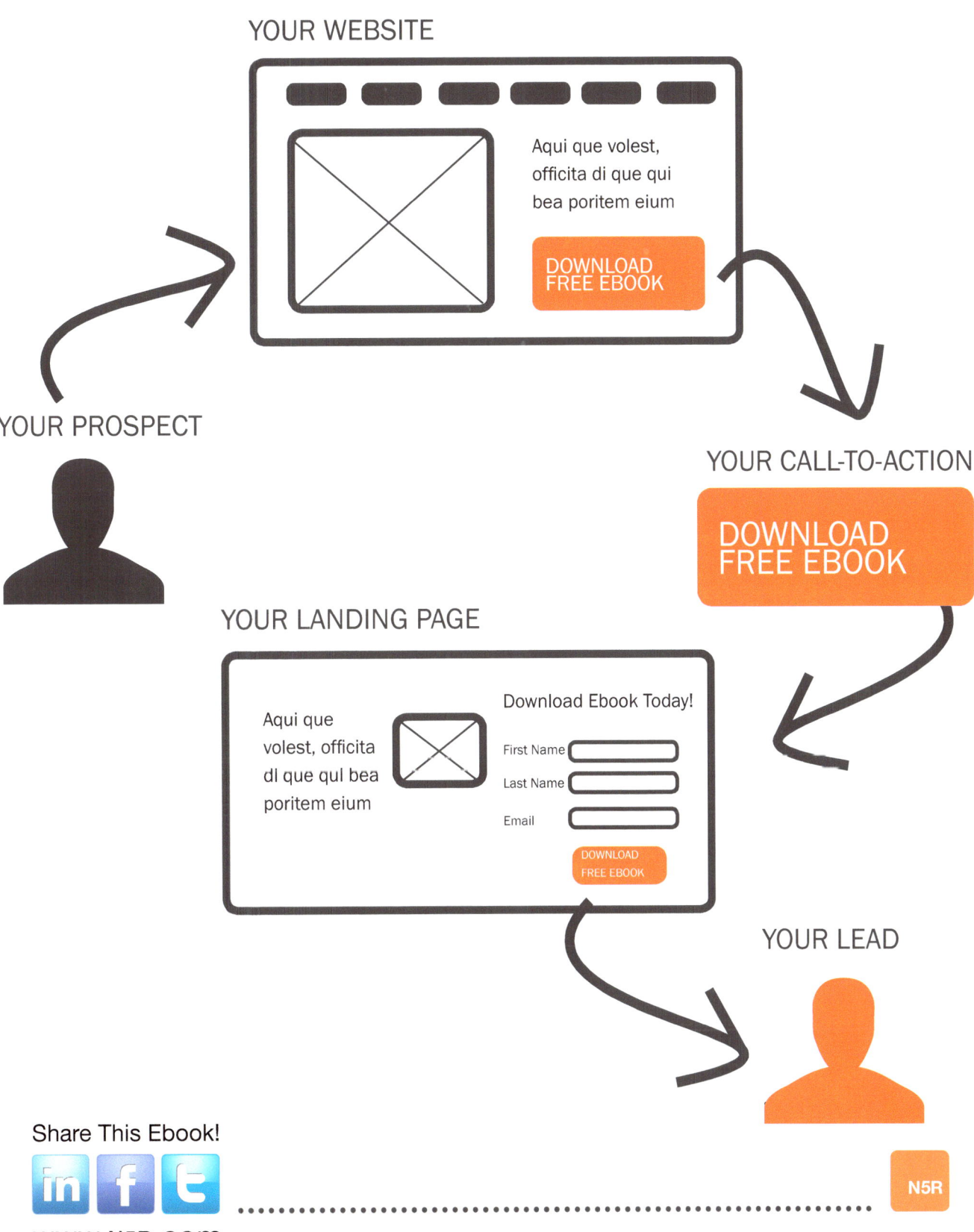

YOUR WEBSITE

Aqui que volest, officita di que qui bea poritem eium

DOWNLOAD FREE EBOOK

YOUR PROSPECT

YOUR CALL-TO-ACTION

DOWNLOAD FREE EBOOK

YOUR LANDING PAGE

Aqui que volest, officita dl que qul bea poritem eium

Download Ebook Today!

First Name
Last Name
Email

DOWNLOAD FREE EBOOK

YOUR LEAD

Share This Ebook!

WWW.N5R.COM

N5R

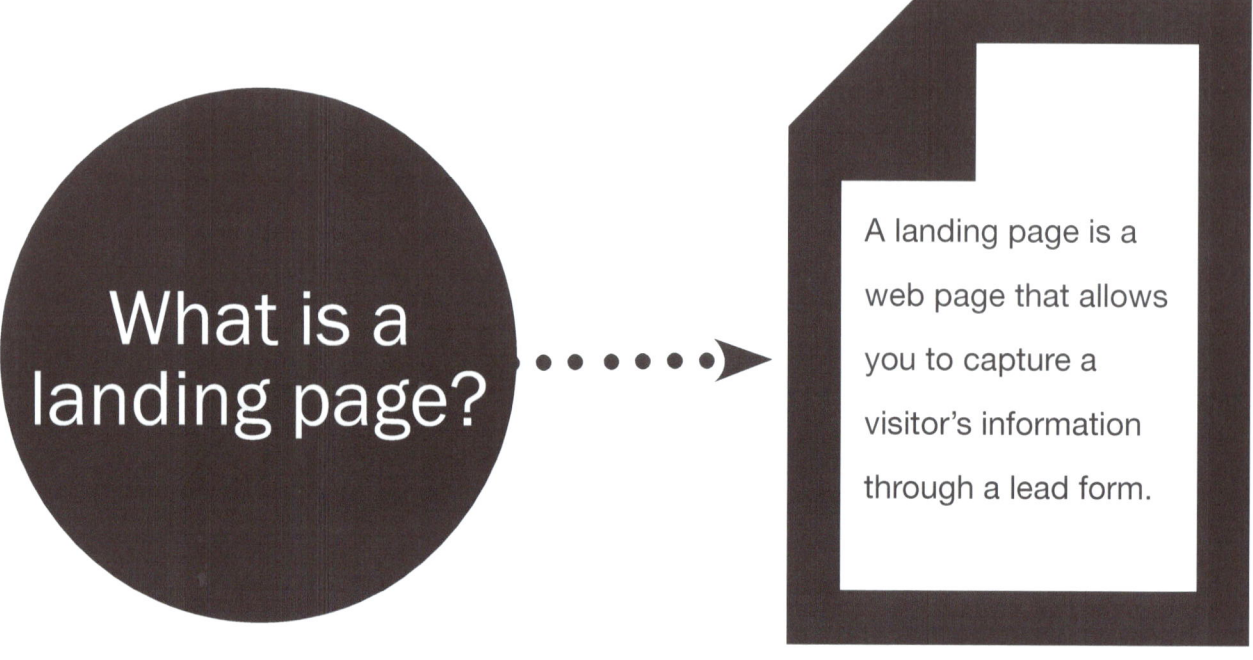

What is a landing page?

A landing page is a web page that allows you to capture a visitor's information through a lead form.

A good landing page will target a particular audience, such as traffic from an email campaign promoting a particular ebook, or visitors who click on a pay-per-click ad promoting your webinar. This is one of the reasons why N5R.com is such an avid supporter of the new HubSpot 3 – the inclusion of A/B Testing give marketers the benefit of choosing the most effective Landing Page version to increase conversion rates, while making unique content more relevant than ever.

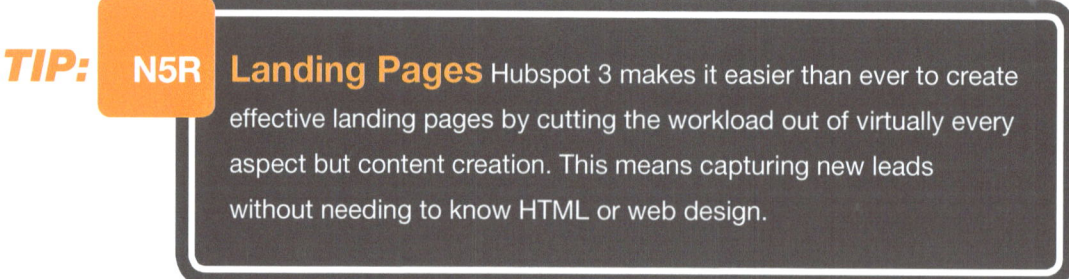

TIP: **N5R** **Landing Pages** Hubspot 3 makes it easier than ever to create effective landing pages by cutting the workload out of virtually every aspect but content creation. This means capturing new leads without needing to know HTML or web design.

Share This Ebook!

WWW.N5R.COM

N5R

Making Your Landing Page Effective

Sure – the built-in tools make it easy to for you to make each element of your *Lovable Marketing* campaign. But remember: a great idea and great content drives your campaign, whether you're doing it in-house or employing the expertise of professional ad marketers.

N5R.com understands what goes into writing great content, and we've updated this checklist for you – some elements to be mindful of when making a landing page to effectively convert a higher percentage of visitors into leads.

● HEADLINE

We all know the common myth: People's attention spans are short, and even shorter online. But what people neglect to append to that, is that attention spans are short when the content is bad. And that's especially true for headlines. So what makes a good headline? Keep it clear, concise, and direct.

Make sure your title makes your offer immediately clear so that the viewer understands what the offer is right away.

> ***TIP:*** **N5R** **SEO writing** "Sales copy" is great for traditional media, but online users typically don't search for marketing sales style queries. If your content is already solid, consider simplifying your headline to something with more search value.

Share This Ebook!

● BODY

The meat of your landing page should say what your offer is and why your visitors should download it or sign up for it. Avoid stating features; highlight benefits instead. Format the body of your page in a way that quickly conveys the value of the offer and the action visitors need to take. Break the text with bullet points and numbering to simplify the visual layout of the text, and use bold or italicized text to highlight the main points.

Share This Ebook!

WWW.N5R.COM

An Example of a Landing Page

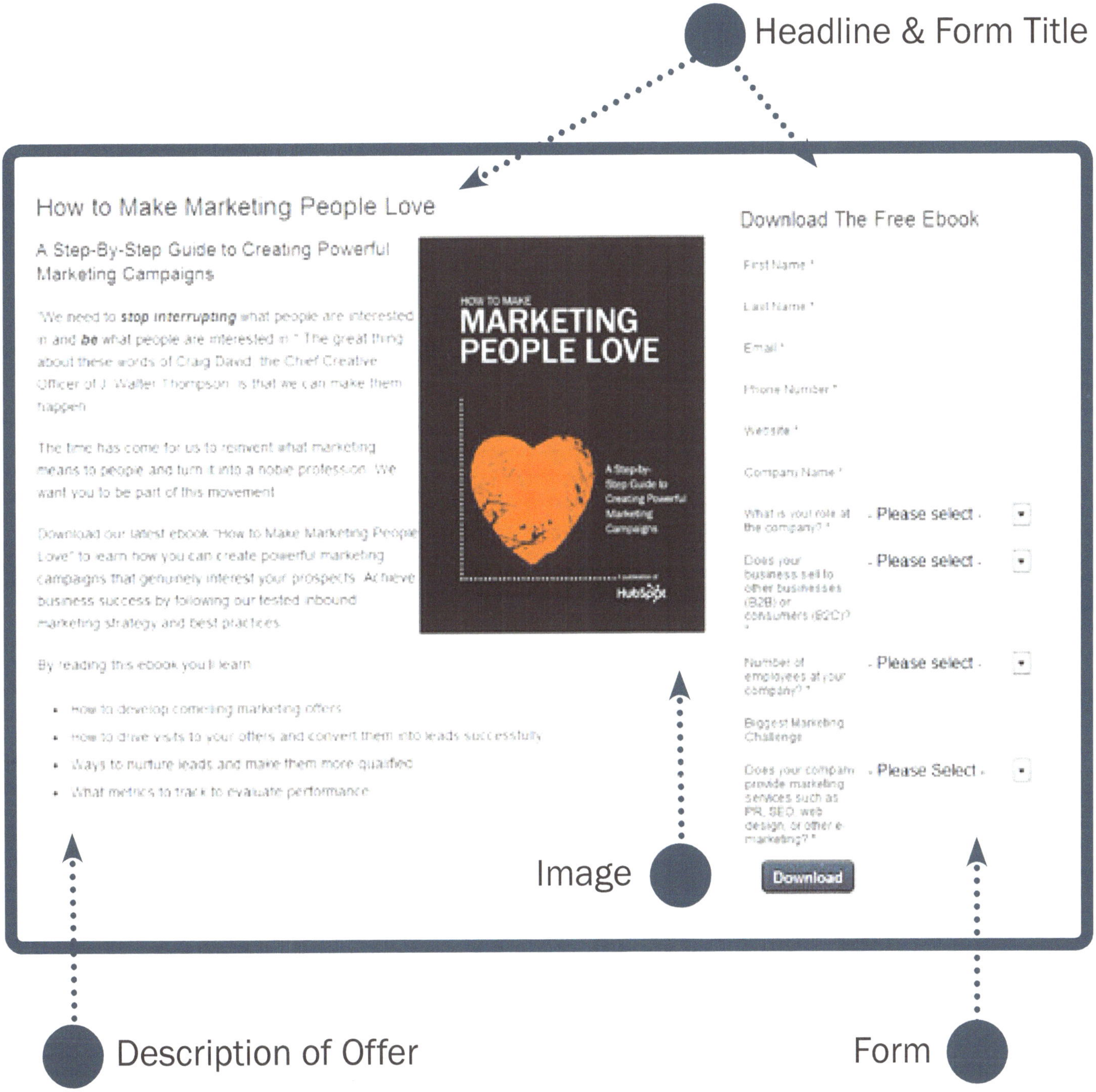

Headline & Form Title

How to Make Marketing People Love

A Step-By-Step Guide to Creating Powerful Marketing Campaigns

"We need to *stop interrupting* what people are interested in and *be* what people are interested in." The great thing about these words of Craig David, the Chief Creative Officer of J. Walter Thompson, is that we can make them happen.

The time has come for us to reinvent what marketing means to people and turn it into a noble profession. We want you to be part of this movement.

Download our latest ebook "How to Make Marketing People Love" to learn how you can create powerful marketing campaigns that genuinely interest your prospects. Achieve business success by following our tested inbound marketing strategy and best practices.

By reading this ebook you'll learn:

- How to develop compelling marketing offers
- How to drive visits to your offers and convert them into leads successfully
- Ways to nurture leads and make them more qualified
- What metrics to track to evaluate performance

MARKETING PEOPLE LOVE

A Step-by-Step Guide to Creating Powerful Marketing Campaigns

HubSpot

Download The Free Ebook

First Name *

Last Name *

Email *

Phone Number *

Website *

Company Name *

What is your role at the company? * - Please select -

Does your business sell to other businesses (B2B) or consumers (B2C)? * - Please select -

Number of employees at your company? * - Please select -

Biggest Marketing Challenge

Does your company provide marketing services such as PR, SEO, web design, or other e-marketing? * - Please Select -

Download

Image

Description of Offer

Form

Share This Ebook!

WWW.N5R.COM

The other critical factor to consider is the effect of the length of the form on the prospect's willingness to fill it out. If the form is too long, prospects are going to stop and evaluate whether it is worth their time to complete all of those fields. So you need to find a good balance between collecting enough information and not asking for too much information that prospects are not willing to give it.

You can avoid dealing with that by booking a meeting with N5R.com to see what we can do for you. Based on N5R.com's experience, once the lead generation of a campaign is tight enough, the length of the form becomes secondary to the quality of the information that the form generates. If you prefer to take a swing yourself, just make sure that the other parts of your campaign are in place to make the most out of your form registrations.

Your goal should be to collect enough information through your form to enable you to contact and qualify the lead. Required fields like name and email address allow you to put them in a workflow and nurture them in the future.

Other required fields include the number of employees, and their role at the company – this lets you qualify the lead and target interactions with them moving forward, to ultimately convert them to a customer.

••••● THE IMAGE

Every landing page built at N5R.com includes a relevant image with a targeted alt attribute. Pages with images – and this is especially true for videos – help retain the focus of leads who land on your page. This is particularly important if copy is sparse (although N5R.com recommends to prioritize copy whenever possible).

The image featured needs to represent the offer you are presenting. For instance, depending on what your offer is, you could feature an image of the cover page of an whitepaper or ebook, or headshots of webinar presenters.

WWW.N5R.COM

N5R

THE FORM

Remember that the ultimate goal of your landing page is to get people to fill out your form. Make sure that your form appears above the fold so that the viewer does not have to scroll down on the page in order to see it.

TIP: **Smart Fields** A new time-saving functionality of HubSpot 3 is Smart Fields. It stores the information that your visitors enter in forms so that on their next visit to your site, they don't need to enter it all over again.

The length of your form inevitably leads to a tradeoff between the quantity and quality of the leads you generate. Shorter forms usually result in more leads, but longer forms will result in fewer, but higher quality leads.

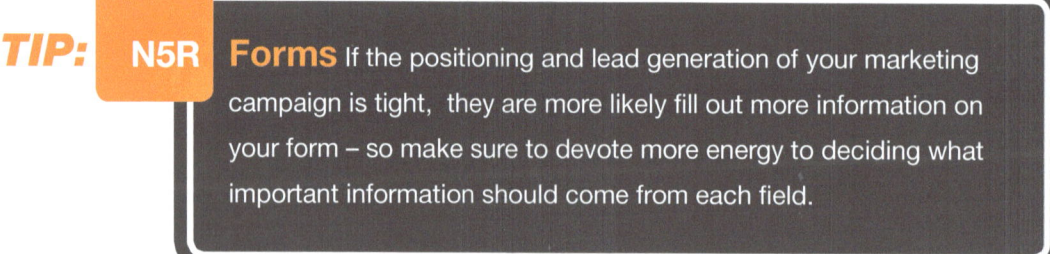

TIP: **N5R** **Forms** If the positioning and lead generation of your marketing campaign is tight, they are more likely fill out more information on your form – so make sure to devote more energy to deciding what important information should come from each field.

Share This Ebook!

   ••••••••••••••••••••••••••••••• **N5R**

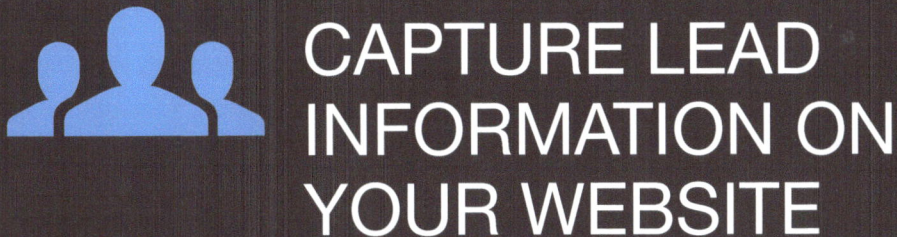

CAPTURE LEAD INFORMATION ON YOUR WEBSITE

Research shows that companies with 30 or more landing pages generate seven times more leads than those with fewer than 10. Hubspot makes it easy to build sophisticated landing pages so you can create more pages, improve your conversion rates and generate more leads.

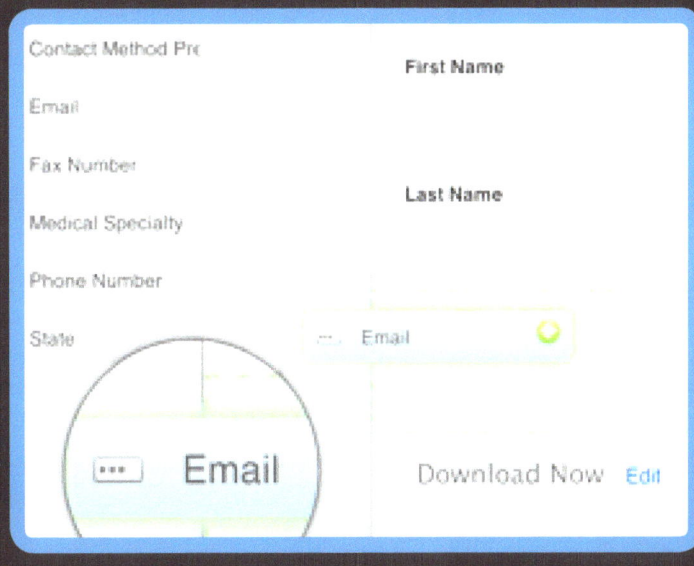

✔ Customizable lead capture forms and auto-response emails.

✔ Built-in call-to-action (CTA) builder.

✔ CRM integration for closed-loop reporting.

✔ Integration with email and lead nurturing.

Request a Demo

Read More

❝ *Make your landing page visible on your website through a call-to-action.* **❞**

•••

Now that you have built a landing page for your offer, you want to make it visible on your website. You can achieve that through a call-to-action.

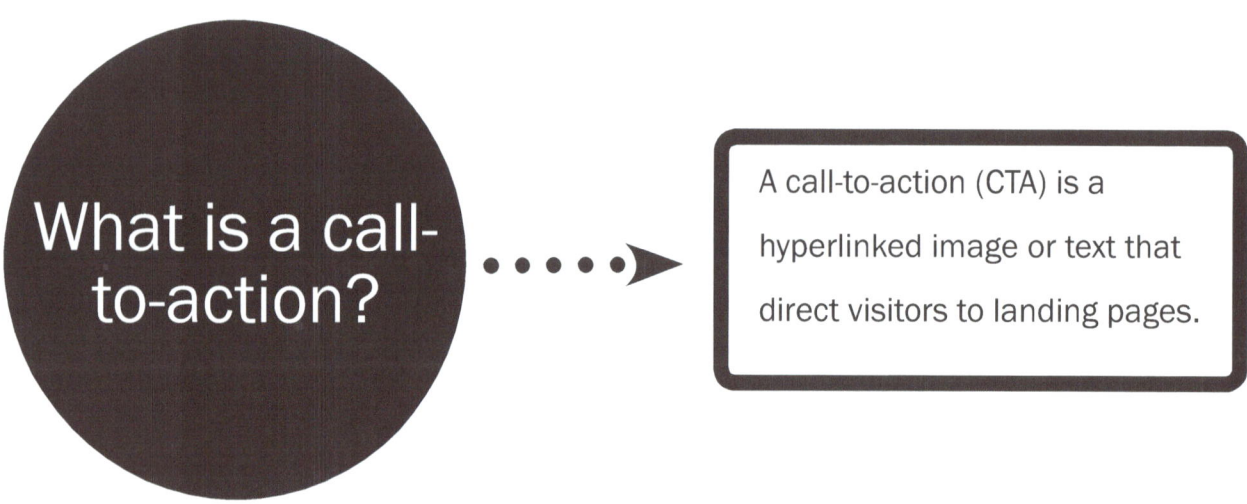

What is a call-to-action?

A call-to-action (CTA) is a hyperlinked image or text that direct visitors to landing pages.

The goal of a call-to-action is to drive traffic to a landing page. In order to increase visitor-to-lead conversion opportunities, you need to create a lot of calls-to-action, distribute them across your web presence and optimize them.

Share This Ebook!

Examples of Calls-to-Action

Free Ebook: 101 Examples of Effective Calls-to-Action

Download Now

Join Cyndi at The World's Largest Gathering of Inbound Marketers

Register Today

GET IN TOUCH   **VIEW OUR WORK**

Get Started

Share This Ebook!

 •••••••••••••••••••••••••••••••••••••••

www.N5R.com

Where should you place your calls-to-action?

Placement is one of the most critical elements of leveraging the power of calls-to-action. So how do you decide which call-to-action belongs where? Simple. Calls-to-action should be spread across your web pages.

Aqui que volest, officita di que qui bea poritem eium di que qui bea

DOWNLOAD FREE EBOOK

Your homepage should have a call-to-action. As your most frequently visited page, your homepage presents a huge opportunity to drive traffic to a specific campaign.

Share This Ebook!

   •

Your Product/Service pages, About Us page and Contact Us page all need to include calls-to-action or the visitor will be deciding on their own what to do next. You need to help them decide what to do next. In fact...

❝ *Every page on your site should help visitors understand what they should do next...*❞

... and therefore, include at least one call-to-action.

TIP: **N5R** **Website Navigation** At N5R.com, we make every effort to see things from our clients' perspective. This means seeing all the angles in order to best decide how to integrate social media platforms into your campaign. Visitors to your website should find exactly what they want in as few clicks as possible. Make sure all your web pages are organized in a clean navigation bar, either running horizontally on the top or vertically down the left. Your call-to-action should be consistently apparent on all pages no matter where your navigation points them.

In all of your marketing assets you should be trying to drive people to get further engaged with your company. If the goal of a call-to-action is to drive traffic to your landing page, think about the different ways in which you can achieve that. For instance, you can use marketing emails and social media updates to drive traffic to your landing page.

Share This Ebook!

CHAPTER 3

BUILD WORKFLOWS

" *Understand the nuances of your leads' timing and needs* **"**

So you have designed a stellar marketing offer and placed it on your website. But before you start driving traffic to it, you need to consider how you are going to nurture the new leads that you create. How are you going to further educate them about your

company and product or service? You will need to use workflows.

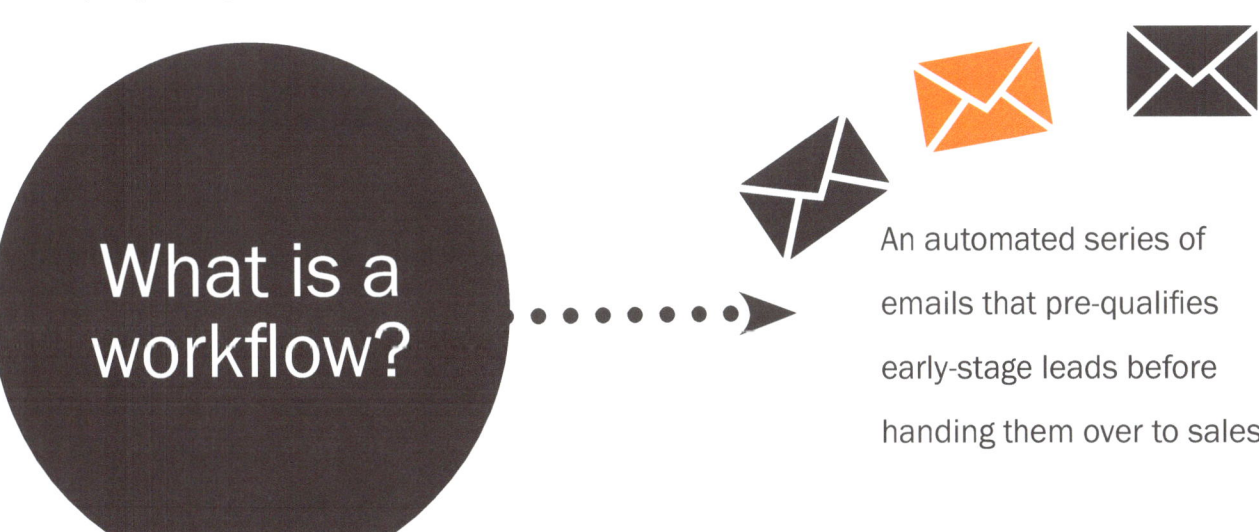

What is a workflow?

An automated series of emails that pre-qualifies early-stage leads before handing them over to sales.

Workflows are also known as advanced lead nurturing, marketing automation, drip marketing, and auto-responders. Their goal is to make your new leads more sales-ready.

Share This Ebook!

The Value of Workflows

Only **5% - 25%** of the traffic on your site is **ready to do businesses** with you at that moment.

THE REST ARE DOING RESEARCH.

#1

25-50% of sales go to the vendor that responds **first**.

Share This Ebook!

WWW.N5R.COM

Confused by the technicality? Wincing at the workload? Don't worry – N5R.com gets it. We know that the power of HubSpot comes packaged with a learning curve – you know how it can save your sales organization time, but you aren't exactly sure how to set it all up. It's okay. We'll do it for you.

Using workflows and nurturing your leads carries a whole bunch of benefits, including:

● TIMELY COMMUNICATION

Study after study shows that email response rates decline over the age of the lead. In his Science of Timing research Dan Zarrella, HubSpot's Social Media Scientist, discovered that there is a positive correlation between subscriber recency and clickthrough rate, one of the key metrics of engagement.

● AUTOMATION

Once you set up workflows, emails are sent out automatically according to your schedule as new leads come in. You might launch the campaigns and forget about them, but the emails will be doing the work for you, helping you qualify leads and push them down the sales funnel faster.

● TARGETING

Studies show that targeted and segmented emails perform better than mass email communications. Lead nurturing enables you to tie a series of emails to a specific activity or conversion event.

Share This Ebook!

SAVE TIME BY AUTOMATING YOUR MARKETING IN AN INBOUND WAY

Marketing automation helps businesses drive revenue by converting more leads into customers. Even the most qualified leads take time to develop, and often move at different speeds. Use Hubspot's workflows app to warm up leads with a series of customized emails based on their activity on your site.

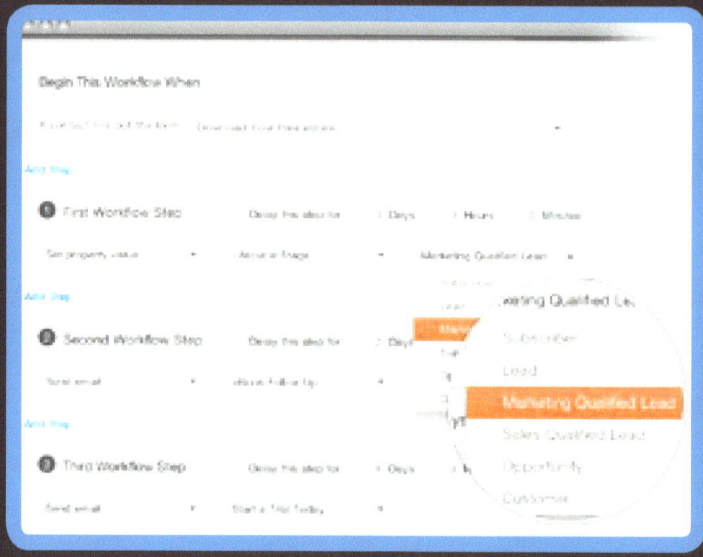

✔ Automatically trigger times follow-up emails.

✔ Trigger personalized emails based on your leads' behavior.

✔ Use automated workflows to update a contact's profile information and lifecycle stage.

✔ Use workflows to add or remove contacts from custom segments.

Request a Demo

Read More

Segmentation Ideas

Your contacts are not all the same. In order to do effective, targeted marketing, you need to break your contact database up into smaller groups or segments.

Creating smaller segments allows you to group your contacts by their interests, industries, geographies, etc., and then create experiences and messages specifically for each segment.

For instance, you can automatically segment your leads based on:

••••● A CONTACT PROPERTY

Based on company name, state, size, industry, lead grade or lifecycle stage, etc.

••••● A FORM SUBMISSION

Based on ebook download, a webinar registration, a demo request, etc.

••••● AN EXISTING LIST

Based on presence in an existing marketing list.

All these are types of segmentation that N5R.com can help your business achieve, so inquire about a 30-day trial, and you can start experimenting with these options immediately.

Share This Ebook!

   ••••••••••••••••••••••••••

WWW.N5R.COM

Making Lead Nurturing Lovable

Still with us? Good. We're at the half way point, and N5R.com will help you through the rest. Then we'll start building your campaign.

After we segment your leads, N5R.com will figure out how we can help move them through your sales and marketing process in a way that caters to their needs. Remember, Lovable Marketing has to be:

•••••••• ● RELEVANT

•••••••• ● TIMELY

•••••••• ● SCALABLE

N5R.com will ensure that your campaign will resonate with each segment. We will update your leads in real-time, nurture them down the sales funnel, and set-up workflows to manage that process. Here's the beautiful thing: we can set-up the workflows to kick-in automatically for each lead once they've been segmented.

That's what HubSpot calls a smart list. So, if someone downloads an ebook, indicates their company size is between 50-200 employees, and says that they are in the manufacturing industry, we can send them your nurturing campaign designed just for them. If another company downloads the same ebook, but says their company size is between 1-10 employees in the software industry, we'll send them a different nurturing campaign more relevant for their business.

Share This Ebook!

   ••••••••••••••••••••••••••••••••••

WWW.N5R.COM

Examples of Workflows

Workflows can be as simple or complicated as we make them. And that's the key point: we design them. Here are some examples of hypothetical workflows that can help you with lead scoring and moving prospects down the sales funnel, accordingly:

1 **WORKFLOW FOR GENERATING A CUSTOM LEAD SCORE:**

STEP 2

Lead receives a score of 20 points.

Visitor requests a consultation with sales.

STEP 1

Person visits your website.

2 WORKFLOW FOR GENERATING SALES:

STEP 4

Leads receives a custom invitation for a free consultation with sales.

STEP 3

Lead is assigned a lifecycle stage.

STEP 2

Lead receives a follow-up email with the requested ebook.

Visitor downloads an ebook.

STEP 1

Person visits your website.

Share This Ebook!

WWW.N5R.COM

N5R

CHAPTER 4

MARKET OFFER TO EXISTING CONTACTS

❝Notify your existing contacts about your new marketing offer. Start with an email announcement.❞

Now that we have ensured that all new prospects who grab your marketing offer will receive the appropriate follow-up communication, let's start thinking about sending traffic to your landing page.

N5R.com suggests to start by thinking about the ways to notify your existing contacts about the new marketing offer you have released. You should begin by immediately turning to your email list – you've spent all this time building it and maintaining it, so let's make use of it.

So how would you go about making this announcement to your email list?

Share This Ebook!

Dedicated Email Send

The best way to get a lot of traffic to your new landing page is to send a dedicated email.

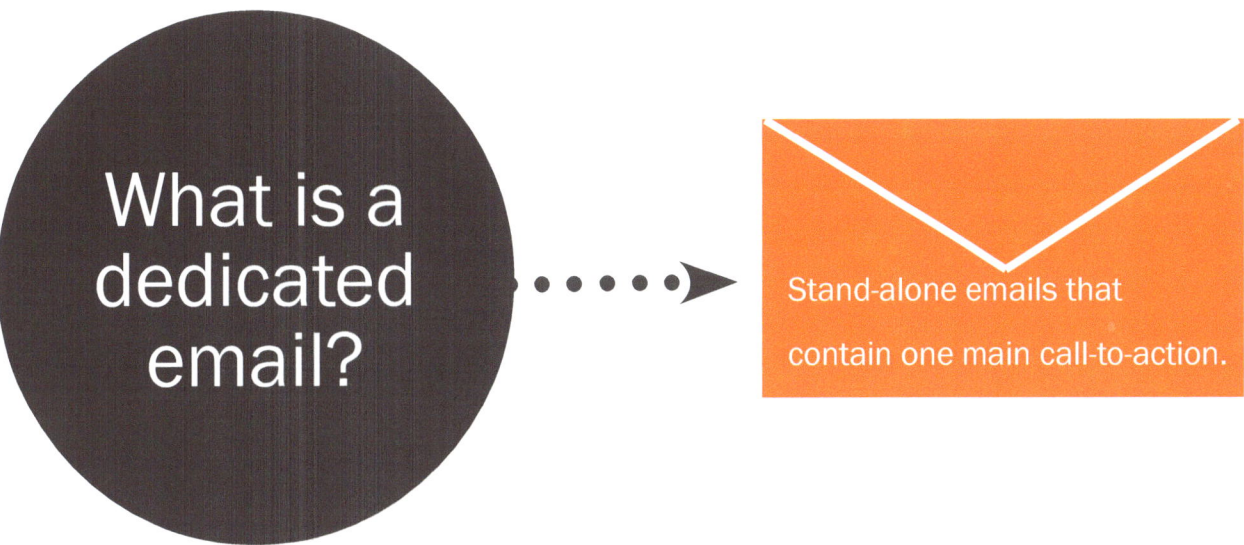

What is a dedicated email?

Stand-alone emails that contain one main call-to-action.

For instance, you can be notifying your target audience about a new whitepaper you have released or invite them to attend an event that you are hosting. Dedicated emails help you set up the context to introduce the main call-to-action.

Dedicated sends can be used to reach out to your entire email database or just a segment that you think this marketing offer applies to.

While there are instances when all of your subscribers should be notified about a specific marketing campaign, such as a timely new offer or an upcoming event, in most cases you would want to segment heavily based on your subscribers' persona.

Share This Ebook!

 ••••••••••••••••••••••••••••••••••••••

WWW.N5R.COM

SEND THE RIGHT MESSAGE AT THE RIGHT TIME TO THE RIGHT LEADS

Email marketing is a valuable tool for educating your leads and helping you stay top-of-mind when they're ready to buy. Hotspot's Email Marketing app allows you to create valuable content that your prospects will look forward to receiving.

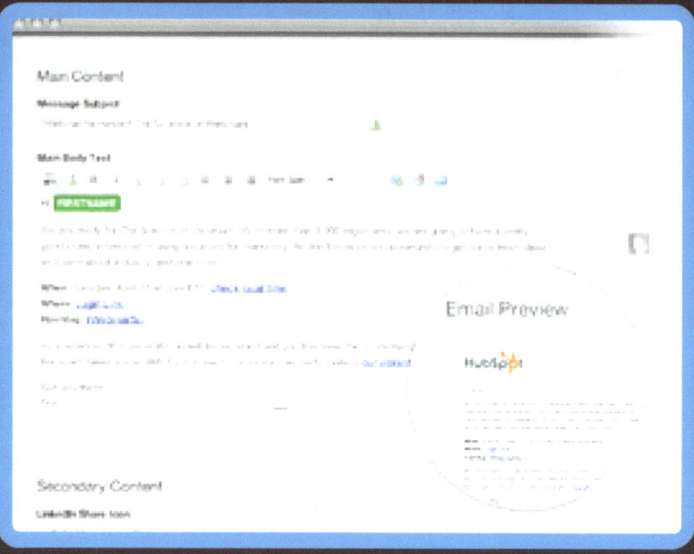

✔ Send personalized, beautiful emails to increase open and click through rates.

✔ Measure which messages are most effective with our robust analytics and reporting tools.

✔ Integrate your messages seamlessly with our Social Media and SEO apps to help you get the most out of your marketing.

Request a Demo

Read More

Tips for Your Email Send

Dedicated email sends are generally easy to set up and measure. Here are some of the things that we at N5R.com keep in mind when we craft your dedicated email:

••••● FEATURE ONE CALL-TO-ACTION

Dedicated sends focus on driving results for one call-to-action. As a Marketing Sherpa case study of Kodak's successful list growth tactic explains, "These calls-to-action were not stuffed at the end of a newsletter or tacked onto another message. They were the focus of a dedicated email, which gave them much more impact."

••••● PERSONALIZE EMAILS

Show your prospects that you know them. N5R.com has developed personalized direct mails, reminder emails, and even video emails on behalf of our business clients, with great success. We can attest to the fact that personalized emails work because they demonstrate a deeper relationship with your audience. And when that happens, they respond time and time again. Just make sure to use a consistent voice across your marketing communication.

••••● DESIGN MOBILE EXPERIENCES

Make sure your email layout displays well on mobile devices. Optimizing for mobile will become important as more people check their emails on their smartphones.

Share This Ebook!

•• N5R

WWW.N5R.COM

● MAKE EMAILS SOCIAL AND SEO-FRIENDLY

You know those Facebook and Twitter buttons on your favorite web pages? Add the buttons to your email so your recipients can share them. Also, make sure that your emails create a web-only version which will ensure you are leveraging your email for SEO.

● CLONE & REUSE

The ability to create an email template, reusing some of the information already on your landing page, and tweaking it to reflect your killer subject header lets us do our job that much easier.

● DESIGN MOBILE EXPERIENCES

Naturally, if you have one main message and call-to-action in your dedicated send, it will be easy for you to track progress. You can quickly check the email CTR, landing page views and conversions, and follow the long-term ROI.

Share This Ebook!

CHAPTER 5

PROMOTE OFFER THROUGH BLOGGING & SOCIAL

"Blogging & social media provide more opportunities to drive traffic to your landing page."

Now that you have announced the release of your new marketing offer to existing contacts in your email database, you can start looking for other opportunities to drive traffic to your landing page. This is where you can leverage your blog and social media channels.

After 14 years of doing online marketing at N5R.com, this is still the part where we have the most fun.

Why is it so great? Because the opportunities we get to interact with our leads and customers are potentially limitless. That means it's very important that the message N5R.com sends on behalf of your business has to be perfect.

Now that you have announced the release of your new marketing offer to existing contacts in your email database, you can start looking for other opportunities to drive traffic to your landing page. This is where you can leverage your blog and social media channels.

After 14 years of doing social media marketing at N5R.com, this is still the part where we have the most fun.

Why is it so great? Because the opportunities we get to interact with our leads and customers are potentially limitless. That means it's very important that the message N5R.com sends on behalf of your business has to be perfect.

TIP: **N5R** **Social Media - YouTube** Arguably the second largest search engine (next to that Google guy), and the best video resource for consumer reviews for products and services. Branding a Youtube channel allows businesses to deliver promo content, and – perhaps more importantly – respond to anti-brand videos before they go viral.

Share This Ebook!

www.N5R.com

How to Use Your Blog in the Campaign

Maintain a blog can be difficult. HubSpot 3 makes it that much easier to manage, but for an organization that already has its hands full, a better alternative would be to get an experienced company to manage it for you.

When putting your blog post together, N5R.com focuses on optimizing the content for humans and search engines. We also make sure to introduce a call-to-action to your marketing offer. (Did we already mention that's important? We did? Awesome.) Here are some more blog tips to get you thinking:

● FEATURE A COMPELLING IMAGE

Include an image that conveys what the blog post is about. This helps maintain the interest of readers and is especially useful where there's a lot of important text. An image could be a graphic, a photograph, or some type of infographic to help pace your content.

● WRITE AN EYE-CATCHING SUBJECT LINE

We at N5R.com hinted to this earlier about subject headers for emails, and the same applies to blogs. Headlines are the most important element of your blog posts. It's what your users see first. While there are quite a few elements that go into a successful blog post, one of the best

Share This Ebook!

things you can do to capture readers' attention and entice them to view your post is to write an awesome blog title.

● FORMAT

Online reading is not like reading a physical book. As a consistent blogger ourselves, we at N5R.com know that the online reader often evaluates an entire website at a glance before deciding whether to keep reading or hit the back button. Looks do matter, after all. So at N5R.com, we can make yours look as good as your content... which we would be writing for you anyway. (See where we're going with this?)

● SOCIAL MEDIA SHARING

Give your blog content extended reach by including social sharing buttons (e.g. "Like," "Share on LinkedIn," "Tweet," etc.) on every post. This will encourage readers to share your content with their personal networks and expand its reach beyond your own connections.

Share This Ebook!

WWW.N5R.COM

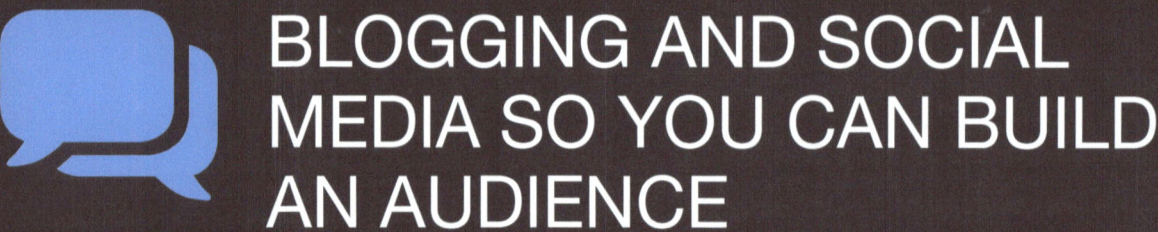

BLOGGING AND SOCIAL MEDIA SO YOU CAN BUILD AN AUDIENCE

Hubspot'vs blogging software, social media tools and website management system make it easy to create remarkable content that will help you get found.

✓ Blogging Software and Analytics: Create and measure your blog.

✓ Social Media Monitoring and Publishing: Track mentions and schedule posts.

✓ Social Media Analytics: See how social media efforts are paying off.

Request a Demo

Read More

How to Use Social in the Campaign

While Twitter, Facebook, LinkedIn, Google+ and Pinterest are all different social media platforms, they have something fundamental in common: the element of information exchange. So with the creation of a good marketing offer to promote, you make your job on social media much easier because now you have content to share! Here are some other best practices when it comes to promoting your marketing offer through social media channels:

•••• ● PLAN THE TIMING OF YOUR PROMOTION

Control how often you share your offers to ensure your account doesn't turn into a spam-bot. This will be contingent upon your business. For example, a recruiter will be more likely to repeatedly share offers to job openings because users will naturally be vested in that opportunity. However, users may not be as willing to download the same whitepaper about, for instance, improving heating systems.

•••• ● DECIDE ON WHICH NETWORKS YOU WILL FOCUS

There are a lot of available social networks out there. Which one are you going to use to promote your offer? You probably don't have bandwidth to spend equal time on all of them. Look at your marketing analytics and your historical performance with different social channels. Identify the three networks that bring you the best results and focus on using them for supporting your campaign.

Share This Ebook!

 •••

TIP: N5R Social Media - Facebook A far cry from its early closed-book days, Facebook allows users the opportunity to share their favorite online content amongst their own networks. Consider integrating a brand page on Facebook to optimize your company reach.

● MAP DIFFERENT CONTENT BASED ON THE NETWORK

Different social networks are effective at promoting different types of content. While visual content performs well on Pinterest and Facebook, simple copy works well for Twitter and LinkedIn. YouTube, on the other hand, is a strictly video sharing platform. Find out which social network makes the most sense for the type of marketing offer you have created.

TIP: N5R Social Media - LinkedIn While optimizing your content for different social media, be mindful of the demographic that each platform represents: LinkedIn, for example, is naturally suited for marketing to other businesses.

Share This Ebook!

USE A HASHTAG

When promoting your offer on Twitter and/or Google+, consider using a hashtag. There's more to hashtags than simply adding a pound sign in front of a word. In fact, simply adding a hashtag to a tweet isn't going to give you any results; you need to integrate them to a marketing campaign.

TIP: **N5R** **Social Media - Twitter** A well-maintained brand page on Twitter can help drive traffic to your landing page. Like Youtube, Twitter is another crucial touch-point where businesses can resolve anti-brand statements in real-time.

As you develop your marketing offer, think of what hashtag would be relevant to this new resource. Try to use the hashtag on the landing page, your marketing emails and, of course, in your social media updates. That will help streamline a lot of the discussions around the offer and help you receive feedback.

TIP: **One-Stop Social Media & Analytics Hub**
With its new social media tracking system and intuitive analytics tools, HubSpot 3 allows you to manage all your social media outlets in one easy-to-use interface. You can even view your ROI for each outlet – without having to switch programs.

Share This Ebook!

WWW.N5R.COM

N5R.com CASE STUDY:
Social Media Client: Platinum Investment Real Estate Group™

In a 2012 campaign for Platinum Investment Real Estate Group™, N5R.com was tasked with an online marketing challenge: how to increase the exposure and visibility of a dedicated group of financial professionals who needed to keep up with competitors' online marketing efforts?

What N5R.com did: leveraged expertise in social media marketing by creating accounts on Twitter and Facebook, and executing a Facebook ad campaign that exposed the client to millions of social media users.

The result: Platinum Investments gained 500 Facebook followers and new leads on the most viewed and effective internet marketing channels today.

Get in touch with N5R.com at www.n5r.com or call us toll free 1.877.502.2028 to experience the same results today.

Share This Ebook!

WWW.N5R.COM

CHAPTER 6

MEASURE EVERY ELEMENT OF YOUR CAMPAIGN

"*Revisit each element of the campaign and how it performed individually and as a part of a whole.***"**

Now that N5R.com has guided you through the process of creating a Lovable Marketing campaign from start to finish, it's time to talk about campaign assessment. Suppose you came to us for a free website evaluation at N5R.com– these are the steps we'd be taking to measure how your campaign performed, individually and as a whole.

Among the wide range of metrics available to us, we would first take a look at the analytics tied to the landing page that hosts your marketing offer.

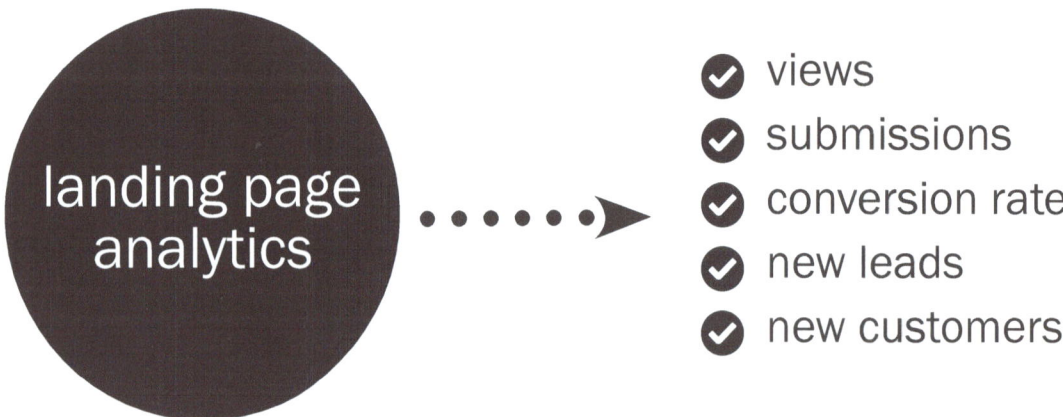

landing page analytics

- ✓ views
- ✓ submissions
- ✓ conversion rate
- ✓ new leads
- ✓ new customers

WWW.N5R.COM

What if Your Performance Was Poor?

If your performance was poor, N5R.com would offer to perform an audit for you to find out exactly which metric needs to be improved. Here some of the things we would look for:

●••••• ● **If the number of views** the landing page got is low, you need to work harder at promoting the offer and sending more traffic to it.

●••••• ● **If the conversion rate** of the landing page is low, you need to focus on creating a more compelling offer or optimizing your landing page.

●••••• ● **If the number of new leads** this offer brought you slow, it could mean that your existing contacts are not sharing your offer with new people. You need to either incentivize them or find venues of promotion to a new audience.

●••••• ● **If the number of customers** the offer brought you isn't very high, that could mean your workflows aren't successful at qualifying leads to convert them into customers. You might need to revise the workflows and make them more powerful.

MARKETING ANALYTICS TO MAKE YOUR SALES FUNNEL MORE EFFICIENT

Hubspot's software tracks all of your marketing activities and automatically generates rich reports so you can spend less time waiting for your pivot tables to load and more time doing real marketing.

✔ Closed-Loop Reporting: Tie your leads back to a specific marketing initiative and calculate your marketing ROI.

✔ Website Analytics: Analyze your Web traffic and see which sources are generating leads.

✔ Competitor Tracking: Analyze your competitors' online metrics.

Request a Demo

Read More

What if Your Performance Was Poor?

N5R.com recommends that when analyzing the rest of the marketing components used in your campaign, start by exploring the number of new leads and customers you generated from each channel. How do they stand up to key performance indicators?

When it comes to calls-to-action, for instance, there are two key metrics we can monitor in order to improve the effectiveness of this marketing asset:

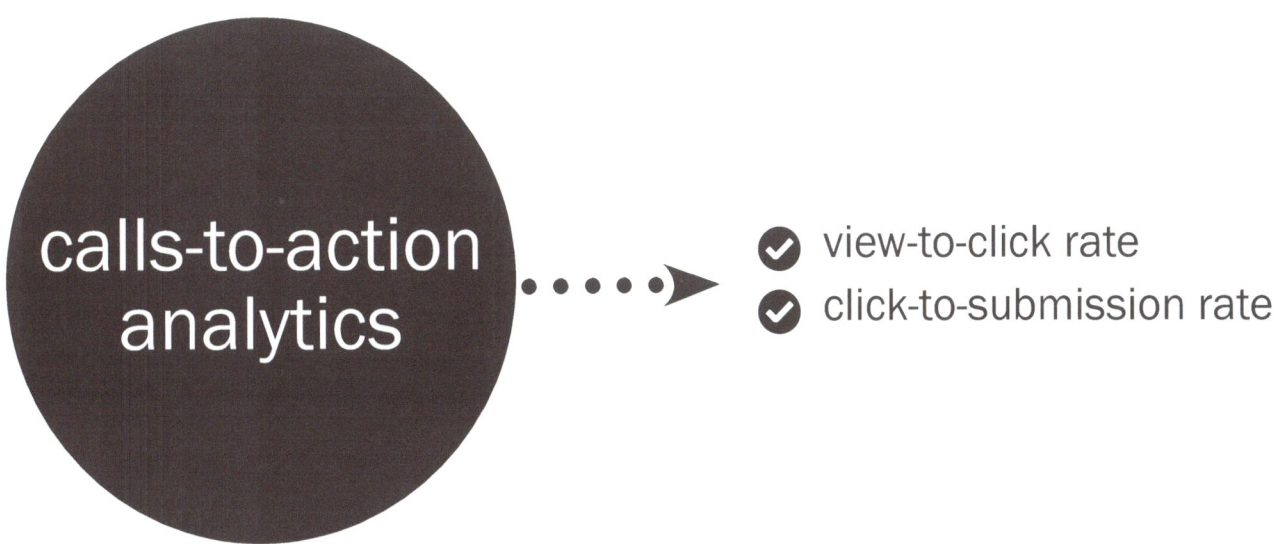

calls-to-action analytics

✓ view-to-click rate
✓ click-to-submission rate

•••••● **If the view-to-click rate** of your calls-to-action is low, make your offer more compelling so that more of the people who see the CTA, click through.

•••••● **If the click-to-submission rate** of your calls-to-action is low, focus on optimizing your landing page and making it perfectly aligned with your CTA.

Share This Ebook!

WWW.N5R.COM

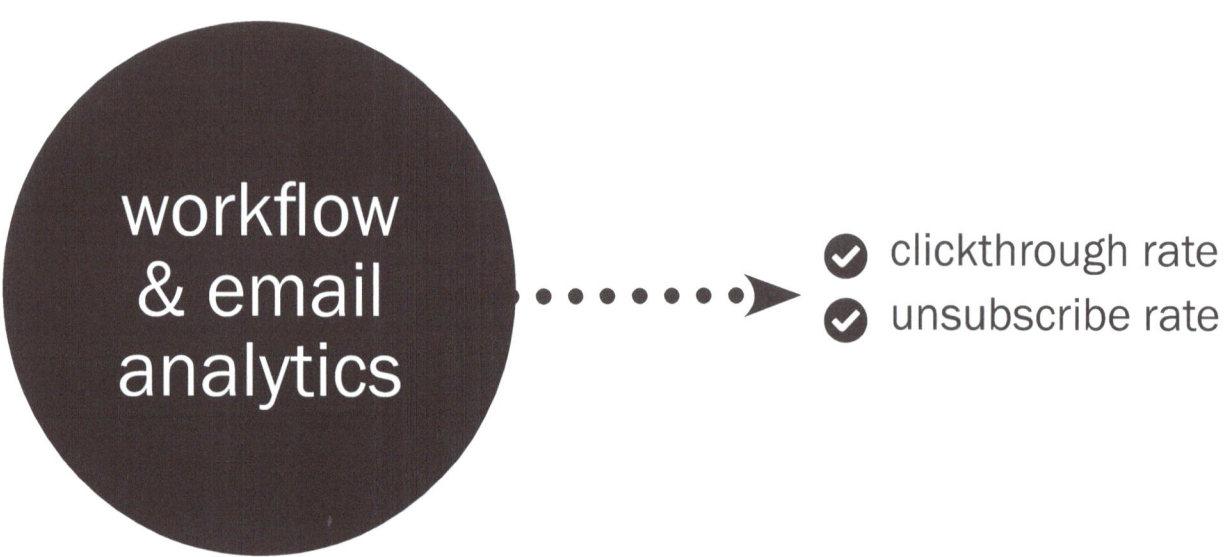

workflow & email analytics

- ✓ clickthrough rate
- ✓ unsubscribe rate

The metrics behind lead nurturing and email marketing overlap. They show the performance of your email sends and the extent to which recipients engage with your email content.

● **If the clickthrough of** your emails is low, that could mean your offer isn't appealing enough to the recipients you are sending it to. Start creating more compelling offers or spend more time on segmentation. (Note that open rate might be a helpful metric, but isn't very reliable.)

● **If the unsubscribe rate of** your emails is low, think carefully about whether the people you are emailing have formally subscribed to receive your email communication. Maybe you need to revise your opt-in procedure or be more precise about setting expectations.

Share This Ebook!

WWW.N5R.COM

N5R

In an N5R.com audit, here are some more key metrics that we bring to your attention when it comes to blogging and social media marketing.

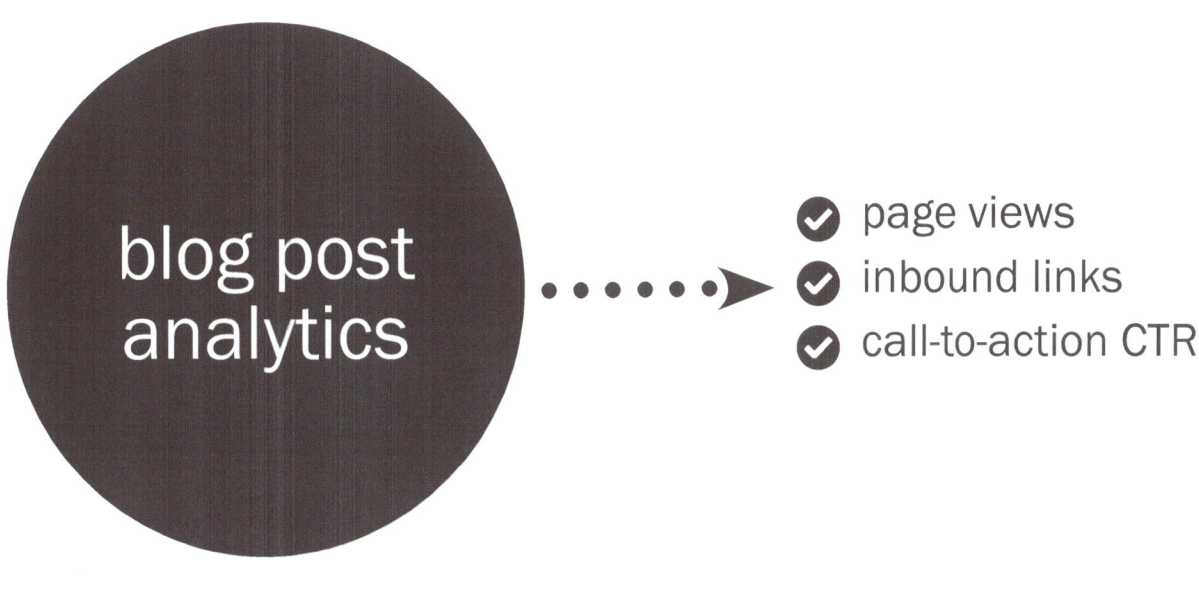

blog post analytics

- ✓ page views
- ✓ inbound links
- ✓ call-to-action CTR

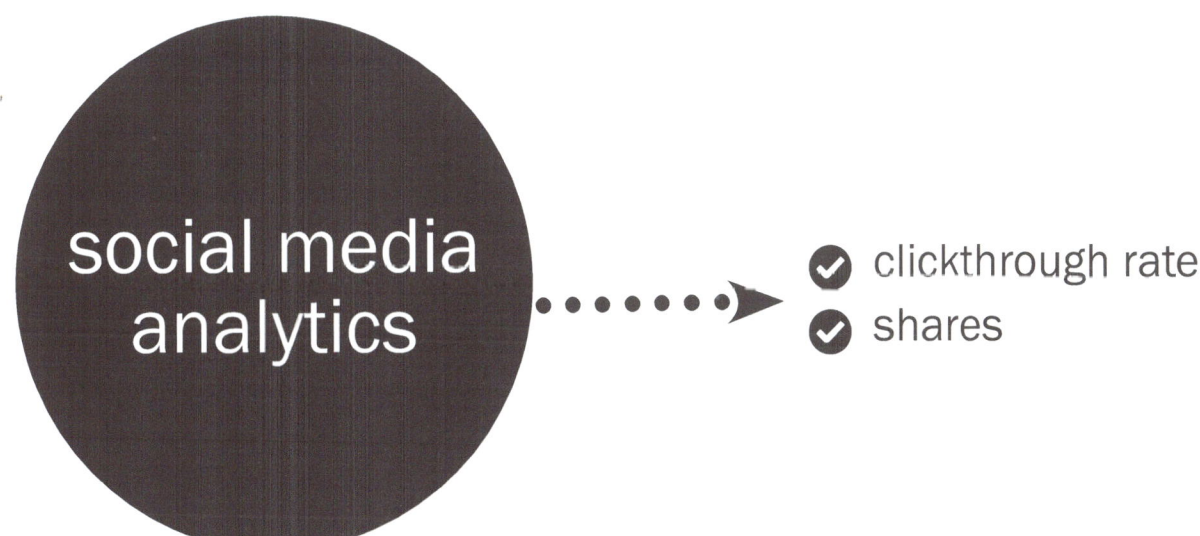

social media analytics

- ✓ clickthrough rate
- ✓ shares

Each metric helps you identify weaknesses and strengths in your marketing campaign. However, don't forget about the bigger picture and stay focused on the number of new leads and customers that your campaign (and each of your channels) generates. Hubspot's marketing analytics gives you access to the number of submissions, new leads and customers you drove by source.

HubSpot 3 makes it easy to look at metrics and analytics, but it's how you interpret the data that really matters. That level of analysis can take years of experience to hone, so when you depend on N5R.com to manage your online marketing efforts on your behalf, rest assured – we've done this before. Lots of times.

Share This Ebook!

 ••• N5R

WWW.N5R.COM

CONCLUSION & ADDITIONAL RESOURCES

"*Now you know how to create a lovable marketing campaign that will bring you lots of new leads and customers.*"

Starting with producing a stellar marketing offer, through promoting it on your channels, to measuring its impact, you have learned how to piece together the main components of a holistic marketing campaign. Most importantly, you know how to make each of these components valuable, consistent and timely – all prerequisites for creating marketing that your prospects will love.

You've made it! And with N5R.com's help, you now have an idea of how SEO and social media outlets occupy an important space in your holistic marketing campaign.

Share This Ebook!

WWW.N5R.COM

Now here's the next step: inquire for a FREE HubSpot 3 Trial at www.n5r.com or by calling 1-866-611-6268 and see for yourself how powerful of a tool this can be in the right hands.

Play with the software. Understand what you want from it. Think about how it can help make your marketing lovable. Then, visit www.n5r.com to let us know exactly what you need done for your campaign.

I would love to hear your marketing challenges to see if we can help you solve them.

Sincerely,

Roman Bodnarchuk

CEO, N5R.com

(416) 220-5314

roman@n5r.com

Share This Ebook!

www.ingramcontent.com/pod-product-compliance
Lightning Source LLC
Chambersburg PA
CBHW050942200526

45172CB00020B/494